A Day with a Mail Carrier

By Jan Kottke

Welcome Books

Children's Press
A Division of Grolier Publishing
New York / London / Hong Kong / Sydney
Danbury, Connecticut

Photo Credits: Cover and all photos by Thaddeus Harden
Contributing Editor: Jennifer Ceaser
Book Design: Nelson Sa

Visit Children's Press on the Internet at:
http://publishing.grolier.com

Library of Congress Cataloging-in-Publication Data

Kottke, Jan.
    A day with a mail carrier / by Jan Kottke.
    p. cm. — (Hard work)
    Includes bibliographical references and index.
    Summary: Explains in simple terms some of the duties of a mail carrier.
    ISBN 0-516-23090-5 (lib. bdg.) — ISBN 0-516-23015-8 (pbk.)
    1. Letter carriers—United States—Juvenile literature. [1. Letter carriers. 2.
Occupations.] I. Title.

HE6499.K68 2000
383'.145'02373—dc21

                                                            00-023357

Contents

1   Meet a Mail Carrier   4

2   Loading the Mail   8

3   Mail to Pick Up   14

4   An Important Letter   16

5   New Words   22

6   To Find Out More   23

7   Index   24

8   About the Author   24

My name is Dominic.

I am a **mail carrier**.

My job is to bring mail to people.

UNITED STATES
POSTAL SERVICE

5

I start my day at the **post office**.

I get to the post office early to sort the mail.

I **load** the mail into my mail truck.

There is a lot of mail today!

8

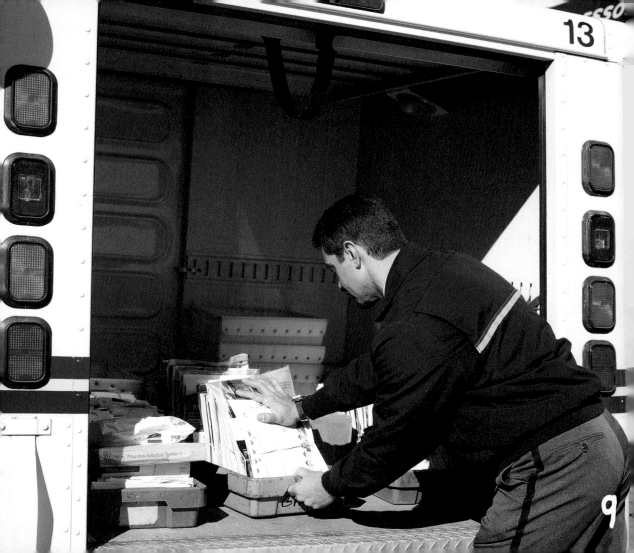

I park my mail truck on the street.

I put some of the mail in my **mail cart**.

I put cards in the **mailbox**.

I put letters in the mailbox.

12

The red flag on this mailbox is up.

It tells me that there is mail to pick up.

443

Some letters are important.

I ring the **doorbell** to let the person inside know.

Sometimes I hand people their mail.

I stop and say "Hello."

19

I like bringing mail to people.

I like being a mail carrier.

21

New Words

doorbell (**dor**-bel) a bell that is rung to
let someone know that you are there

load (**lohd**) put into

mailbox (**mayl**-boks) a box where mail
is placed

mail carrier (**mayl kayr**-ree-er) a
person who brings and picks up mail

mail cart (**mayl kart**) a bag with
wheels used to hold mail

post office (**pohst aw**-fis) a place
where mail is sorted

22

To Find Out More

Books

The Post Office Book: Mail and How It Moves
by Gail Gibbons
HarperCollins Children's Books

Where Does the Mail Go?: A Book About the Postal System
by Melvin Berger and Gilda Berger
Hambleton-Hill Publishing

Web Site
United States Postal Service
http://www.usps.gov
The official site of the United States Postal Service. It has lots of information about the post office.

23

Index

doorbell, 16

letters, 12, 16
load, 8

mailbox, 12, 14
mail carrier, 4, 20
mail cart, 10
mail truck, 8, 10

post office, 6

About the Author
Jan Kottke is the owner/director of several preschools in the Tidewater area of Virginia. A lifelong early education professional, she is completing a phonics reading series for preschoolers.

Reading Consultants
Kris Flynn, Coordinator, Small School District Literacy, The San Diego County Office of Education

Shelly Forys, Certified Reading Recovery Specialist, W.J. Zahnow Elementary School, Waterloo, IL

Peggy McNamara, Professor, Bank Street College of Education, Reading and Literacy Program